Self-Love Journal

Praise for Self-Love Journal:
12 Ways To Love Yourself Like God Wants You To

"I was challenged to think about how forgiving I am and how much hindrance the act of unforgiveness has been in some of my relationships. The last but certainly the most important thing I experienced was the need to seek God for answers to questions I couldn't readily answer or answers that didn't align with his character. Hence, highlighting my need to "pray, pray and pray some more."

-**Jodie McGregor,** Residential Appraiser, Silver Spring, MD

" I love what you've done and felt like I was listening to a friend…it's warm and non-judgmental. It feels like the reader is talking to a sister-friend in a loving way about experiences we've all had and then you provide practical steps for moving forward, supported by the Word."

-**Wendy Hill,** Former Civil Servant, Montgomery County, MD

"It's easy to read, flow is natural. I especially like that it is not churchy-everyday language and easy to understand."

-**Tammie Williams,** Retired Litigation Claim Specialist, Laurel, MD

"I often struggled with how to pray and what to ask for. I know now that having a conversation with God does not have to be filled with elaborate phrases. This journal identifies in simple terms what to pray for and how powerful prayer can be. Forgiving myself is BIG! Every time I mess up I have to forgive myself and realize I am an imperfect human being. Readers delving into this journal will really stop and reflect on what it means to be on their own side and uncover true self love. 12 Ways To Love Yourself Like God Wants You To is soul reflecting, life changing and life affirming."

-**Taundra Hurt,** Director of Operations, Central Islip, NY

Self-Love Journal

12 Ways To Love Yourself Like God Wants You To

Cheryl Latney Bridges

Self-Love Journal: 12 Ways To Love Yourself Like God Wants You To

Trade Paperback ISBN: 979-8-218-01123-9

Published in the United States by ISLM Publishing

Table of Contents

Introduction

● ● ● ● ● ● ● ● ● ● ● ● ● ● ●

Self-love is a journey that requires being on your own side. You may wonder what that looks like. I hope as you continue reading, you'll develop your perspective of what it means to be on your own side.

For me, it means to love God while loving who He fearfully and wonderfully created me to be. It means embracing self-love, self-care, and putting myself at the top of my priority list. It means experiencing joy, peace, and contentment in who I am and where I am. It means accepting who I am – flaws and all. It means trusting that I am enough and have always been enough because of Him.

Being on your own side can be quite a journey. A journey is no more than traveling from one place to another, right? It seems straightforward, however, I'm here to declare the journey to self-love, self-care, and self-respect is anything but straight. My journey was what inspired me to pen this journal. Life experiences. Revelations. Spiritual awakenings. Each of these moments in time created opportunities for growth and development, opportunities for an exciting journey from learning myself to loving myself.

As you travel alongside me throughout the steps in this book, you'll discover the impact journeying from one place to another has on your life. You'll begin to identify with the significance of "being on your own side." You'll learn the importance of self-love, understanding that loving yourself makes it easier to love others. Jesus commands us in Matthew 22:37-39 to *"Love the Lord your God with all your heart and with all your soul and with all your mind. This is the first and greatest commandment."* And the second is like it: *"Love your neighbor as yourself."*

As you read and meditate on the passages in this book, I pray that it will become one of the most important resources you'll ever read during your journey to self-love.

Let's begin the journey!

Step 1
There to Here: Making the Connection

● ● ● ● ● ● ● ● ● ● ● ● ● ● ●

Growing up in Southern New Jersey, my mother often told my brother and me: "I don't care who did what to whom, but you'd better stop that fighting right now!" It was not difficult to guess the outcome if we continued to disobey her order.

In our adult life, making those connections is not always as obvious. Life's past experiences (and behaviors that persist into the present) shape our ability (or inability) to connect the dots. Situations such as negative thinking patterns, childhood trauma, fear, and worry can contribute to low self-esteem, resulting in a lack of love for self.

I believe that moving from there to here is virtually impossible without first establishing the starting point – where is "there?" The question 'where am I going?' remains unclear if not first connected to the question of 'where am I?' These questions can be easily translated to, "who am I?" and "who do I want to be?" Not having the answers can result in feelings of confusion, uncertainty, and doubt.

Over the past several years, I have invested a great deal of time learning about temperament and its effects on who we are and why we act the way we do. Identifying our God-given, inborn temperament is another means of gaining insight into questions

3

such as: "Why do I overthink everything?" "Why do I worry so much?" "Why am I so hard on myself?" And the list goes on and on. God created all of us with temperament strengths, weaknesses, and needs. When we are operating outside of our God-given, inborn temperament, it creates stress and anxiety. Becoming more accepting of ourselves enables us to love ourselves exactly the way God created us to be. David said in Psalms 139:14: *"I praise you because I am fearfully and wonderfully made; your works are wonderful; I know that full well!"*

Creating connections in my relationships with God, with myself and with others was a critical factor on the path to self-love. During this journey, I learned that truly loving myself the way God wanted me to involved creating boundaries, releasing anger, shifting attitudes, facing truths, forgiving, and so much more.

Reflection Questions for the Journey

1) In what ways can you become more accepting of yourself and of others?

_____
_____
_____
_____
_____
_____
_____
_____
_____
_____
_____
_____
_____
_____
_____
_____
_____
_____
_____
_____
_____
_____
_____
_____
_____
_____
_____

2) Which of the relationships mentioned on page 4 (God, self and others) require more of your attention?

_____
_____
_____
_____
_____
_____
_____
_____
_____
_____
_____
_____
_____
_____
_____
_____
_____
_____
_____
_____
_____
_____
_____
_____
_____
_____
_____
_____
_____
_____
_____
_____

Step 1

Scriptures to Guide Your Self-Love Journey

You are altogether beautiful, my love; there is no flaw in you.
Song of Solomon 4:7 (ESV)

Above all, keep loving one another earnestly, since love covers a multitude of sins.
1 Peter 4:8 (ESV)

There is no fear in love, but perfect love casts out fear. For fear has to do with punishment, and whoever fears has not been perfected in love.
1 John 4:18 (ESV)

I praise you because I am fearfully and wonderfully made; your works are wonderful; I know that full well!
Psalms 139:14 (NIV)

For we are his workmanship, created in Christ Jesus for good works, which God prepared beforehand, that we should walk in them.
Ephesians 2:10 (ESV)

Step 2
Prayer to Purpose: The Impact of Persistent Prayers

● ● ● ● ● ● ● ● ● ● ● ● ● ● ●

Have you ever tried to follow your GPS for directions, and it seemed to have you making lefts, then rights, and maybe even U-turns? Well, that's exactly what you may experience on the journey to self-love and self-discovery. You may go right, back up, make a U-turn, and start all over! And that's okay.

So many of us struggle with questions like: "Who am I?" "Why am I here?" "What is God's calling on my life?" The answer is not always packaged precisely as we envisioned. The solution does not always come in neatly organized steps. But I believe sincere and focused prayer, guided by His Holy Spirit, can get us on our way.

I've discovered the best way to begin the journey is by loving God and loving your neighbor as yourself. After all, how can you love your neighbor if you don't love yourself? Making yourself a priority begins with understanding who you are so you can become who you want to be.

I'd like to suggest four steps to begin this journey:

Step 1: PRAY for His PLAN

Ask God to show you His plan for your life. Before following Christ, I trusted my own instincts and developed an "I can do" attitude. It seemed my instincts were leading to an excellent plan for my life. I had good friends, a husband, children, a great career, and good health. As I matured, I realized my life lacked substance, conviction, and genuine faith. We must allow His plan to take precedence, and He will reveal it at just the right time.

Step 2: PRAY for PREPARATION

Ask God to prepare you, but I must warn you that the preparation step can be painful. My "I can do" attitude seemed to work just fine for most of my life. But one fateful day, the unimaginable happened. Something that I could not fix. My father was diagnosed with a malignant glioma, a type of brain cancer, and given only three months to live. *What? Seriously? No way! This could not be possible... or could it?* I quickly realized I might not be able to fix this one, but I surely tried. I studied, researched, sought second opinions, and still, my father's condition continued to deteriorate. I couldn't fix this one.

During those three months, I consistently heard God's voice commanding me to let go and let Him work. During my father's illness and ultimate passing (exactly three months to the day of his diagnosis), I began to genuinely respond to God's voice through prayer, meditation, and study. I believe He was preparing me for many things to come.

In times like these, He's growing you and equipping you in ways that may not seem reasonable or even fair. But trust Him. He knows what He's doing. And He'll do it at just the right time. Don't get out ahead of Him – let His Spirit lead you.

Step 3: PRAY for PEOPLE

Ask God to send you the right people to pray for you and pray with you. No matter how much confidence you may have in yourself, you still need God to make the right connections with the right people at the right time.

Step 4: PRAY for POWER

Ask God for the power of His Holy Spirit to work within you. God has a way of accomplishing things in you that you can't achieve within your human power.

As you can see, the theme is quite evident: pray, pray, and pray some more. Powerful prayer can move you toward your purpose!

"And pray in the Spirit at all times and on every occasion. Stay alert and be persistent in your prayers for all believers everywhere."
Ephesians 6:18 (NLT)

Reflection Questions for the Journey

1) What do you believe God is preparing you for?

_____

_____

_____

_____

_____

_____

_____

_____

_____

_____

_____

_____

_____

_____

_____

_____

_____

_____

_____

_____

_____

_____

_____

_____

_____

_____

_____

_____

_____

2) How can prayer push you towards your passion and purpose?

_____
_____
_____
_____
_____
_____
_____
_____
_____
_____
_____
_____
_____
_____
_____
_____
_____
_____
_____
_____
_____
_____
_____
_____
_____
_____
_____
_____
_____
_____
_____
_____

Step 2

Scriptures to Guide Your Self-Love Journey

Therefore I tell you, whatever you ask for in prayer, believe that you have received it, and it will be yours.
Mark 11:24 (NIV)

Pray without ceasing.
1 Thessalonians 5:17 (ESV)

And whatever you ask in prayer, you will receive, if you have faith.
Matthew 21:22 (ESV)

And pray in the Spirit at all times and on every occasion. Stay alert and be persistent in your prayers for all believers everywhere.
Ephesians 6:18 (NLT)

And we know that for those who love God all things work together for good, for those who are called according to his purpose.
Romans 8:28 (ESV)

Step 3
Feeling to Forgiveness: Unfinished Business?

● ● ● ● ● ● ● ● ● ● ● ● ● ● ●

A critical part of this journey to self-love must be forgiveness. Forgiveness, however, is a choice. It can be a long and seemingly impossible journey when you've been hurt or betrayed. Allowing yourself to face the feelings that come with any negative emotion is essential to the process.

It's not uncommon to mask our true feelings surrounding hurt. The mask may scream anger when beneath the mask is real pain. It's perfectly acceptable to let your true feelings flow. It's impossible to eliminate all your hurt feelings and negative thoughts – the goal is to change your response to them. Feel the emotion but try not to become the emotion.

Choosing to forgive is a way to release the pain that continuously rears its ugly head from the memory of past incidents. It is also a choice made with much prayer and through the guidance of the Holy Spirit.

Forgiveness is also freedom. It allows you to take your power back. Often, the person or situation towards which you continue to harbor unforgiveness has likely moved on. It's probably time for you to move on, as well. That energy can be used for something positive and productive. Forgiving yourself and others will create the space you need to go from here to there.

"If you forgive the failures of others, your heavenly Father will also forgive you. But if you don't forgive others, your Father will not forgive your failures."
Matthew 6:14-15 (GW)

Reflection Questions for the Journey

1) Who do you need to forgive?

_____
_____
_____
_____
_____
_____
_____
_____
_____
_____
_____
_____
_____
_____
_____
_____
_____
_____
_____
_____
_____
_____
_____
_____
_____
_____
_____
_____
_____
_____
_____

2) What do you need to forgive yourself for?

_____
_____
_____
_____
_____
_____
_____
_____
_____
_____
_____
_____
_____
_____
_____
_____
_____
_____
_____
_____
_____
_____
_____
_____
_____
_____
_____
_____
_____
_____
_____

Step 3

Scriptures to Guide Your Self-Love Journey

Be kind to one another, tenderhearted, forgiving one another, as God in Christ forgave you.
Ephesians 4:32 (ESV)

If we confess our sins, he is faithful and just to forgive us our sins and to cleanse us from all unrighteousness.
1 John 1:9 (ESV)

If you forgive the failures of others, your heavenly Father will also forgive you. But if you don't forgive others, your Father will not forgive your failures.
Matthew 6:14-15 (GW)

Jesus said, "Father, forgive them, for they do not know what they are doing."
Luke 23:34 (a) (NIV)

For if you forgive other people when they sin against you, your heavenly Father will also forgive you. But if you do not forgive others their sins, your Father will not forgive your sins.
Matthew 6:14-15 (NIV)

Step 4
Pity to Power: Exit, Stage Left!

● ● ● ● ● ● ● ● ● ● ● ● ● ●

Have you ever hosted your very own pity party? Were you the host, the guests, and the entertainment? Sometimes, life has a way of knocking us down, and it feels almost impossible to get up. That's okay. It's understandable. Occasionally, attending your own pity party may be just what you need for self-reflection. But take caution not to hang out at the party too long!

If you've never invited yourself to a pity party, kudos to you! But many have attended these parties, and they've lasted days, weeks, or even months! So, what exactly is this pity party all about? It's an unhealthy and unproductive activity in which excessive time is spent with feelings of guilt, shame, fear, and failure while complaining about your current situation without trying to do anything to change it.

Some signs of a pity party may include feelings of sadness, anger, or frustration. It also may involve feeling unmotivated and even binging on television. Excessive negative thinking and complaining seem to be consistently at the top of the list.

Unfortunately, these symptoms can cause difficulties in relationships as those around you may pick up on the negative vibes and cause withdrawal from friendships. The pity party then continues to grow.

To avoid these unfortunate consequences, here are three ways you can exit your pity party and invite yourself (and others) to your very own power party:

Acknowledge and accept your thoughts and beliefs

One way to begin the exodus from your pity party is to become more aware of how your thoughts and beliefs impact your mood and behavior. If you realize negative self-talk has become a habit, it's time to adjust those beliefs and self-talk so that they are more truthful, positive, and optimistic. Start viewing obstacles as opportunities for growth rather than roadblocks.

"Finally, brothers and sisters, whatever is true, whatever is noble, whatever is right, whatever is pure, whatever is lovely, whatever is admirable—if anything is excellent or praiseworthy—think about such things." Philippians 4:8

Affirm who you are

It's important to understand who you are (and whose you are) to envision who you want to become (and who God wants you to be). Affirmations, which are statements said with confidence about a perceived truth, can be powerful in helping you change your mood, thought pattern, or state of mind. Positive affirmations, such as "I am worthy," "I am productive," and "I am blessed" can help you transform pity into power. Speaking the affirmations out loud daily or even writing them out in a journal will allow you to reinforce these new beliefs.

"But by the grace of God, I am what I am, and his grace to me was not without effect."
1 Corinthians 15:10(a)

Aspire to achieve

Now that you've acknowledged your thoughts and affirmed who you are, it's time to achieve. It's time to cancel your RSVP to the pity party. It's critical to set aside negative self-talk, fear, and self-pity and replace those emotions with positivity, productivity, and power. Taking more responsibility for your life and where it's heading will lead you in the right direction. An anonymous writer once said, *"When you want something you've never had, you have to do something you've never done."*

"For the Spirit God gave us does not make us timid, but gives us power, love and self-discipline."
2 Timothy 1:7

Reflection Questions for the Journey

1) What pity party have you been attending for too long?

_____
_____
_____
_____
_____
_____
_____
_____
_____
_____
_____
_____
_____
_____
_____
_____
_____
_____
_____
_____
_____
_____
_____
_____
_____
_____
_____
_____
_____
_____
_____
_____

2) What is your exit strategy?

_____

_____

_____

_____

_____

_____

_____

_____

_____

_____

_____

_____

_____

_____

_____

_____

_____

_____

_____

_____

_____

_____

_____

_____

_____

_____

_____

_____

_____

_____

_____

Step 4

Scriptures to Guide Your Self-Love Journey

"Finally, brothers and sisters, whatever is true, whatever is noble, whatever is right, whatever is pure, whatever is lovely, whatever is admirable—if anything is excellent or praiseworthy—think about such things."
Philippians 4:8 (NIV)

I can do all this through Him who gives me strength.
1 Philippians 4:13 (NIV)

"But by the grace of God, I am what I am, and his grace to me was not without effect."
1 Corinthians 15:10(a) (NIV)

Give thanks in all circumstances; for this is the will of God in Christ Jesus for you.
1 Thessalonians 5:18 (ESV)

Consider it pure joy, my brothers and sisters, whenever you face trials of many kinds, because you know that the testing of your faith produces perseverance.
James 1:2-3 (NIV)

"For the Spirit God gave us does not make us timid, but gives us power, love and self-discipline."
2 Timothy 1:7 (NIV)

Step 5
Hopeless to Happy: Discover You

● ● ● ● ● ● ● ● ● ● ● ● ● ●

Do you ever feel lost and not sure where your life is headed? Do you wish you could find the purpose for your life? It's possible to discover your passion and purpose while identifying your values and what makes you feel fulfilled.

I realized it was time to reflect on what things in life were important to me. What did I value? The obligations and worries of life tended to overpower some of those thoughts, feelings, and dreams. I eventually changed the narrative and began to chart a new path by embracing the God in me.

When I became ready to take my life to the next level, I implemented some self-care practices:

First, I prayed and meditated. During stressful times, I learned to be still and be quiet. It was a healthy way to block out the noise of the world. With practice, I could find peace regardless of what was going on around me.

Then, I did something I loved every single day. Even if it was something that only took a few minutes, I did it. Spending a few precious moments with myself and doing what I loved improved my mood and increased my energy level.

I also began to look for the good. There is typically an opportunity to find something good within every negative situation, but it may require searching for it. I began to open my eyes wide and see the blessings and possible solutions in every case. It was at those points that I found peace.

Finally, I took a self-care vacation. Sometimes, a change of scenery will change your whole perspective. A few days of relaxation allowed me to rest my soul, spirit, mind, and body.

Once I took the time to discover what really mattered to me, I aligned my life in a way that brought meaning to me and those around me.

S – seek to learn all you can about yourself

E – examine your values

L – leverage what you learn

F – focus on what matters most

"Then God's peace, which goes beyond anything we can imagine, will guard your thoughts and emotions through Christ Jesus."
Philippians 4:7 (GW)

Reflection Questions for the Journey

1) What are your favorite ways to take care of yourself emotionally and mentally?

_____
_____
_____
_____
_____
_____
_____
_____
_____
_____
_____
_____
_____
_____
_____
_____
_____
_____
_____
_____
_____
_____
_____
_____
_____
_____
_____
_____

2) What are your values, and in what ways is your life NOT aligned with these values?

_____
_____
_____
_____
_____
_____
_____
_____
_____
_____
_____
_____
_____
_____
_____
_____
_____
_____
_____
_____
_____
_____
_____
_____
_____
_____
_____
_____
_____

Step 5

Scriptures to Guide Your Self-Love Journey

I know what I'm doing. I have it all planned out—plans to take care of you, not abandon you, plans to give you the future you hope for.
Jeremiah 29:11 (MSG)

Peace I leave with you; my peace I give to you.
Not as the world gives do I give to you. Let not your hearts be troubled, neither let them be afraid.
John 14:27 (ESV)

You will keep in perfect peace those whose minds are steadfast, because they trust in you.
Trust in the Lord forever, for the Lord, the Lord himself, is the Rock eternal.
Isaiah 26:3-4 (NIV)

"Then God's peace, which goes beyond anything we can imagine, will guard your thoughts and emotions through Christ Jesus."
Philippians 4:7 (GW)

See what kind of love the Father has given to us, that we should be called children of God; and so we are. The reason why the world does not know us is that it did not know him.
1 John 3:1 (ESV)

Step 6
Fear to Faith: What Are You Really Afraid Of?

● ● ● ● ● ● ● ● ● ● ● ● ● ● ●

Fear – that single emotion that has put limits on me and repeatedly robbed me of peace and joy. Fear, if left unchecked, can be crippling. My brothers and sisters, God wants us to live an abundant life – full of happiness, peace, and love. Ask yourself, "what are you really afraid of?"

Below are personal testimonies and scriptures that helped me move from FEAR to FAITH.

> *"The Lord himself goes before you and will be with you; he will never leave you nor forsake you. Do not be afraid; do not be discouraged."* **Deuteronomy 31:8**

I remember a time when I sat on my bedroom floor, crying out to God. My relationship was in shambles, my 31-year career had ended, and I didn't know which way to turn. My entire life was about to change. I stretched my right hand above my head, and I literally felt God holding my hand. I had never experienced that type of feeling before. At that moment, I knew God was present. He had not left me, nor had He forsaken me. It was so powerful. When you're feeling this way, remember you are NEVER alone. Be still and feel His presence all around you. He's right there with you.

"At the right time, I, the Lord, will make it happen."
Isaiah 60:22(b) (NLT)

Many of my fears came from believing that if it didn't happen in my time, it wouldn't happen at all. Ever. What would I do? I allowed fear to creep in and create anxiety, doubt, and worry. I've come to realize, however, that God will do it. He will make it happen. It may not look the way we envisioned, but He's faithful. God is also the ultimate strategist. It wasn't meant to be if it doesn't happen when we think it should happen. God has a wonderful plan and purpose for your life. Trust Him. He knows what He's doing. There is no reason to fear – He's got an impeccable track record!

"He forgives your sins – every one. He heals your diseases – every one. He crowns you with love and mercy – a paradise crown. He wraps you in goodness – beauty eternal. He renews your youth – you're always young in His presence. God makes everything come out right; he puts victims back on their feet." **Psalm 103:3-6 (MSG)**

God is a promise keeper. Look at all His promises just in these four verses! I was laid off from my place of employment after 31 years of loyal service. Just when I began to get really scared, and I didn't know where to turn, God turned it all around. He was preparing me to walk in my purpose with passion and power. Won't He do it? God has big dreams for our lives, and He wants us to follow Him. Don't be afraid. He keeps His promises, and I'm living proof that God specializes in fixing things.

Reflection Questions for the Journey

1) What are you really, really afraid of?

_____

_____

_____

_____

_____

_____

_____

_____

_____

_____

_____

_____

_____

_____

_____

_____

_____

_____

_____

_____

_____

_____

_____

_____

_____

_____

_____

_____

_____

_____

_____

_____

_____

_____

2) If fear has ever held you back from accomplishing your goals, how can you exercise your faith to move forward?

_____

_____

_____

_____

_____

_____

_____

_____

_____

_____

_____

_____

_____

_____

_____

_____

_____

_____

_____

_____

_____

_____

_____

_____

_____

_____

_____

_____

_____

_____

_____

_____

_____

Step 6

Scriptures to Guide Your Self-Love Journey

When I am afraid, I put my trust in you.
Psalm 56:3 (ESV)

Even though I walk through the valley of the shadow of death, I will fear no evil, for you are with me; your rod and your staff, they comfort me.
Psalm 23:4 (ESV)

So faith comes from hearing, and hearing through the word of Christ.
Romans 10:17 (ESV)

"The LORD himself goes before you and will be with you; he will never leave you nor forsake you. Do not be afraid; do not be discouraged."
Deuteronomy 31:8 (NIV)

"At the right time, I, the Lord, will make it happen."
Isaiah 60:22(b) (NLT)

"He forgives your sins – every one. He heals your diseases – every one. He crowns you with love and mercy – a paradise crown. He wraps you in goodness – beauty eternal. He renews your youth – you're always young in His presence. God makes everything come out right; he puts victims back on their feet."
Psalm 103:3-6 (MSG)

Step 7
Comparison to Confidence: Embracing Your Uniqueness

● ● ● ● ● ● ● ● ● ● ● ● ● ●

In the words of Theodore Roosevelt, *"Comparison is the thief of joy."*

Have you ever found yourself caught in the age-old comparison trap? I know I have. Every time I got caught up, it sucked the energy right out of me! Thus, I began to relate to those famous words from Theodore Roosevelt. I discovered that comparing myself to others stole my joy and destroyed my confidence.

One of the easiest ways to get entangled in the comparison game is to waste valuable time scrolling through social media hour after hour, day after day, week after week. Continually studying the "highlight reels" of the lives of, in many cases, complete strangers is bound to trigger the onset of this energy-draining game.

After getting caught in the trap time and time again, I decided it was time to change the narrative.

First, it became necessary for me to focus on all my many, many blessings. It's easy to forget how God has kept us, blessed us, and repeatedly protected us. I also had to take the focus off ME and place it on serving others. I learned to become more "others-conscious" and less "self-conscious."

Next, I had to flip from negative thinking to positive thinking. When those negative thoughts began to creep in, I reached for the Word. I meditated on Philippians 4:8, which reads: *"Christian brothers, keep your minds thinking about whatever is true, whatever is respected, whatever is right, whatever is pure, whatever can be loved, and whatever is well thought of. If there is anything good and worth giving thanks for, think about these things."*

Then, I decided to concentrate on the facts. The facts are:

> 1) God created me in His image – fearfully, wonderfully, and uniquely;
>
> 2) God has every hair on my head numbered;
>
> 3) God is intimately aware of every one of my gifts, talents, and skills;
>
> 4) God has ordered every single step and created unique opportunities just for me;
>
> 5) God has created assignments that only I can complete.

And the list could go on and on and on.

Finally, I started working out and exercising my faith muscles. When I began to step out on faith, trust God and yield fully to Him, my confidence and self-worth began to soar. I realized that with God, I am enough. I am His child. I am complete in Him. I am His workmanship. I have the mind of Christ. I am redeemed. I am a friend of Christ. I am free. I am confident!

No need for comparison now, is there? Embrace who God created you to be… uniquely you.

"… let's just go ahead and be what we were made to be, without enviously or pridefully comparing ourselves with each other, or trying to be something we aren't."
Romans 12:6-8 (MSG)

Reflection Questions for the Journey

1) When have you fallen into the comparison trap?

_____

_____

_____

_____

_____

_____

_____

_____

_____

_____

_____

_____

_____

_____

_____

_____

_____

_____

_____

_____

_____

_____

_____

_____

_____

_____

_____

_____

_____

_____

_____

2) What are some ways you can modify your behaviors to avoid this trap?

_____
_____
_____
_____
_____
_____
_____
_____
_____
_____
_____
_____
_____
_____
_____
_____
_____
_____
_____
_____
_____
_____
_____
_____
_____
_____
_____
_____
_____
_____
_____
_____

Step 7

Scriptures to Guide Your Self-Love Journey

Therefore do not throw away your confidence, which has a great reward. For you have need of endurance, so that when you have done the will of God you may receive what is promised.
Hebrews 10:35-36 (ESV)

And I am sure of this, that he who began a good work in you will bring it to completion at the day of Jesus Christ.
Philippians 1:6 (ESV)

Finally, brothers and sisters, whatever is true, whatever is noble, whatever is right, whatever is pure, whatever is lovely, whatever is admirable—if anything is excellent or praiseworthy—think about such things.
Philippians 4:8 (NIV)

For the Lord will be your confidence and will keep your foot from being caught.
Proverbs 3:26 (ESV)

…let's just go ahead and be what we were made to be, without enviously or pridefully comparing ourselves with each other, or trying to be something we aren't.
Romans 12:6-8 (MSG)

Step 8
Critical to Contented: The Importance of Gratitude

● ● ● ● ● ● ● ● ● ● ● ● ● ●

To be grateful is to be content. To be content is to be at peace. To find peace is an amazing blessing.

I often reflect on a song I sang in my younger years entitled, "Every day is a Day of Thanksgiving" by Dr. Charles G. Hayes. This song is a frequent reminder of how blessed I am every morning. I'm blessed simply to open my eyes, stand to my feet, walk, move, speak, think, and love.

While the COVID-19 pandemic caused holidays and other major events to look a bit different for our families and friends, there are still so many reasons to be grateful and to glorify our Lord. Be sure to take time to focus on strengthening your faith. By recognizing the many wonderful things God has done for you, your faith grows more and more with every thought.

An attitude of gratitude strengthens our faith muscles and is also a means to maintain positive energy, improve self-esteem, and lower stress. As we have seen in recent months and years, we are in control of very little in this world. Emphasizing what we can control, what we have (and not what we lack), and who we are in

Christ will undoubtedly lead to contentment, gratefulness, and peace.

And let me clarify, contentment doesn't mean I don't want more. It means I am satisfied with where God has me now, and I can wait patiently for Him to reveal what's next.

As I give thanks for all things in all seasons, I also challenge myself to make these six decisions consistently:

T – trust God for all my needs

H – help someone out

A – appreciate what I have

N – notice the beauty of God's creation

K – kindness must be shown to others

S – see the best in everyone

"Actually, I don't have a sense of needing anything personally. I've learned by now to be quite content whatever my circumstances. I'm just as happy with little as with much, with much as with little. I've found the recipe for being happy whether full or hungry, hands full or hands empty. Whatever I have, wherever I am, I can make it through anything in the One who makes me who I am." Philippians 4:11-13 (MSG)

Gratitude, gratitude, gratitude! Practice it. Every day is a day of thanksgiving!

Reflection Questions for the Journey

1) What are you grateful for?

_____

_____

_____

_____

_____

_____

_____

_____

_____

_____

_____

_____

_____

_____

_____

_____

_____

_____

_____

_____

_____

_____

_____

_____

_____

_____

_____

_____

_____

_____

_____

_____

_____

_____

_____

_____

_____

2) How can you practice gratitude daily?

Step 8

Scriptures to Guide Your Self-Love Journey

This is the day that the Lord has made; let us rejoice and be glad in it.
Psalm 118:24 (ESV)

In every way and everywhere we accept this with all gratitude.
Acts 24:3 (ESV)

Give thanks to the Lord, for he is good; His love endures forever.
1 Chronicles 16:34 (NIV)

Actually, I don't have a sense of needing anything personally. I've learned by now to be quite content whatever my circumstances. I'm just as happy with little as with much, with much as with little. I've found the recipe for being happy whether full or hungry, hands full or hands empty. Whatever I have, wherever I am, I can make it through anything in the One who makes me who I am.
Philippians 4:11-13 (MSG)

And whatever you do, whether in word or deed, do it all in the name of the Lord Jesus, giving thanks to God the Father through him.
Colossians 3:17 (NIV)

Step 9
Getting to Giving: The Path to Long-Lasting Joy

● ● ● ● ● ● ● ● ● ● ● ● ● ●

A familiar passage in the Bible, Acts 20:35, tells us, *"It is more blessed to give than to receive."* But do we believe it? How could that be? Getting *feels* so good!

It has become painfully obvious that many of us are more isolated and focused on ourselves rather than others. Seemingly, the world is more and more self-centered. It's no surprise, then, that getting has begun to overshadow giving. Society and culture continue to associate happiness with material possessions when this happiness is only temporary. Giving is so much bigger than this, as it can place us on the path to permanent joy.

Once I committed to bridging the gap from getting to giving, I discovered there are different ways to give (and many of these gifts were free). Giving others mercy, compassion, and kindness resulted in feelings of fulfillment. I have found that focusing more on giving has helped reduce my stress and lessen anxiety. Getting has yet to deliver these same statistics.

What a wonderful gift it has been to give my time and attention to someone who needs it and giving thanks, blessings, and unconditional love doesn't cost a dime.

So, why is it better to give than to receive? Here are a few reasons:

> **G** – God's word says so in Acts 20:35

> **I** – inspiration (your giving will likely inspire others and be an example)

> **V** – value (the recipient of your giving will feel valued, important, and worthy)

> **E** – esteem (improved self-esteem)

Getting to giving…the path to happiness and joy!

Reflection Questions for the Journey

1) How can you experience permanent joy rather than temporary happiness?

_____
_____
_____
_____
_____
_____
_____
_____
_____
_____
_____
_____
_____
_____
_____
_____
_____
_____
_____
_____
_____
_____
_____
_____
_____
_____
_____
_____
_____
_____
_____

2) Think of a situation in which 'giving' created an indescribable feeling of fulfillment for you and how it impacted you moving forward.

_____
_____
_____
_____
_____
_____
_____
_____
_____
_____
_____
_____
_____
_____
_____
_____
_____
_____
_____
_____
_____
_____
_____
_____
_____
_____
_____
_____
_____

Step 9

Scriptures to Guide Your Self-Love Journey

Give, and it will be given to you. Good measure, pressed down, shaken together, running over, will be put into your lap. For with the measure you use it will be measured back to you."
Luke 6:38 (ESV)

May the God of hope fill you with all joy and peace in believing, so that by the power of the Holy Spirit you may abound in hope.
Romans 15:13 (ESV)

These things I have spoken to you, that my joy may be in you, and that your joy may be full.
John 15:11 (ESV)

It is more blessed to give than to receive.
Acts 20:35 (NIV)

Mercy to the needy is a loan to God, and God pays back those loans in full.
Proverbs 19:17 (MSG)

Step 10
Uptight to Unflappable: Are You Emotionally Intelligent?

• • • • • • • • • • • • • •

Many of us struggle with allowing emotions to master our lives rather than becoming the master of our own emotions.

So, what is this emotional intelligence? In my own words, it is simply the ability to manage your emotions to contribute to successful relationships with others. Monitoring your feelings, so they don't control you is an extremely effective way to reduce stress and overcome challenges in your personal life and professional life.

I recently viewed a video of a 29-year-old flight attendant who delivered heartfelt words to passengers during the final moments of her last flying assignment. She was furloughed after two-and-a-half years because of the global pandemic's impact on the airline industry. What is significant about this story is that rather than be angry, agitated, or argumentative about this unfortunate airline decision, she decided to "sign off" with an uplifting, unfeigned, and unflappable message.

This was truly a demonstration of emotional intelligence. The compassion and grace displayed by this young flight attendant is a lesson for us all. Her ability to remain calm as she delivered her remarks while focusing on the positives and expressing gratitude to the airline (the same airline that let her go) for her two-and-a-half-year career is highly commendable.

My first step in developing emotional intelligence was identifying my stressors and the situations that caused me to react rather than respond. Being in tune with these stressors helped me quickly manage the stress and keep ahead of the game. Practicing empathy, expressing gratitude, and learning to manage negative emotions were all critical in developing emotional intelligence.

As my emotional intelligence increased, I found I could build stronger relationships, succeed at work, and achieve my goals in life. Emotional intelligence helped me understand who I am so I could be who I wanted to be. Demonstrating a higher level of emotional intelligence serves me well in every aspect of life.

The question to be considered is: can emotional intelligence be learned, or is it inborn? Well, psychologists are still not sure whether adults can enhance their emotional intelligence or not. However, current research suggests that people can almost surely increase their emotional competence. But I know from personal experience that it takes time, practice, intentionality and help from his Holy Spirit.

"But the fruit of the Spirit is love, joy, peace, patience, kindness, goodness, faithfulness, gentleness, self-control; against such things, there is no law."
Galatians 5:22-23 (ESV)

Reflection Questions for the Journey

1) In what situations have you been successful at managing your emotions?

_____
_____
_____
_____
_____
_____
_____
_____
_____
_____
_____
_____
_____
_____
_____
_____
_____
_____
_____
_____
_____
_____
_____
_____
_____
_____
_____
_____
_____
_____

2) Many human beings struggle with overcoming either anger or fear. Which one of these emotions do you struggle with most? What are some things you can do to begin to face these emotions rather than ignore them?

_____

_____

_____

_____

_____

_____

_____

_____

_____

_____

_____

_____

_____

_____

_____

_____

_____

_____

_____

_____

_____

_____

_____

_____

_____

_____

_____

_____

_____

_____

Step 10

Scriptures to Guide Your Self-Love Journey

A hot-tempered man stirs up strife, but he who is slow to anger quiets contention.
Proverbs 15:18 (ESV)

Like a city whose walls are broken through is a person who lacks self-control.
Proverbs 25:28(NIV)

Let the peace of Christ rule in your hearts, since as members of one body you were called to peace. And be thankful.
Colossians 3:15 (NIV)

But the fruit of the Spirit is love, joy, peace, patience, kindness, goodness, faithfulness, gentleness, self-control; against such things, there is no law.
Galatians 5:22-23 (ESV)

Don't hit back; discover beauty in everyone. If you've got it in you, get along with everybody. Don't insist on getting even; that's not for you to do. "I'll do the judging," says God. "I'll take care of it."
Romans 12:17 (MSG)

Step 11
Perplexed to Pellucid: The Path to Your Purpose

● ● ● ● ● ● ● ● ● ● ● ● ● ●

According to Webster's Dictionary, perplexity is bewilderment, and pellucidity means easy to understand.

It would be amazing to wake up one morning and realize that you are no longer bewildered or perplexed about your purpose in life! As great as that sounds, it's not always the case for everyone. If you find you still struggle to find your God-given purpose, you are not alone.

The path to my purpose began to form about ten years ago while participating in a discipleship program entitled <u>MasterLife</u>. The participants were charged with finding their "life purpose scripture." This pursuit involved much prayer and even more patience.

For most of my life, I've always had a heart for helping people and a genuine concern for the well-being of others. Showing mercy and compassion towards others always seemed to show up very naturally. While praying for God to reveal a scripture that would align with my spiritual gifts of exhortation, mercy, and helps, He led me to Philippians 2:3-4 (MSG): *"Don't push your way to the front; don't sweet-talk your way to the top. Put yourself aside, and help others get ahead. Don't be obsessed with getting your own advantage. Forget yourselves long enough to lend a helping hand."*

And just like that, God's Word revealed my passion, and my passion led me to my purpose of helping others realize their full potential so they become the best version of themselves God would have them to be.

What has become clear to me now is realizing our purpose doesn't solely involve materialistic possessions. While our purpose may need to align with a way to earn money to provide for ourselves and our families, our passions (things that make us feel satisfied, fulfilled, and valued) should also be considered.

Ultimately, I believe our purpose in life is to bring glory to God by using the gifts, talents, and skills he has uniquely provided to each of us. The apostle Paul tells us in Ephesians 2:10, "We are God's handiwork, created in Christ Jesus to do good works, which God prepared in advance for us to do." He has gifted us with all we need to fulfill our purpose.

Take time to get "quiet" with the Lord. Spend time in prayer, in meditation, and in His word. Consider meditating on scriptures to lead you to your life purpose. Proverbs 19:21 says: *"Many are the plans in a person's heart, but it is the Lord's purpose that prevails."* God's plans for us are so much better than we could ever imagine. Listen for His voice. Be prayerful and be patient.

Following God's will for your life will move you from perplexity to pellucidity!

Reflection Questions for the Journey

1) What do you believe you are called to do?

_____
_____
_____
_____
_____
_____
_____
_____
_____
_____
_____
_____
_____
_____
_____
_____
_____
_____
_____
_____
_____
_____
_____
_____
_____
_____
_____
_____
_____
_____
_____
_____

2) What are some ways you can gain clarity around your calling?

_____
_____
_____
_____
_____
_____
_____
_____
_____
_____
_____
_____
_____
_____
_____
_____
_____
_____
_____
_____
_____
_____
_____
_____
_____
_____
_____
_____
_____
_____

Step 11

Scriptures to Guide Your Self-Love Journey

And we know that for those who love God all things work together for good, for those who are called according to his purpose.
Romans 8:28 (ESV)

But seek first the kingdom of God and his righteousness, and all these things will be added to you.
Matthew 6:33 (ESV)

But it is the spirit in man, the breath of the Almighty, that makes him understand.
Job 32:8 (ESV)

Don't push your way to the front; don't sweet-talk your way to the top. Put yourself aside, and help others get ahead. Don't be obsessed with getting your own advantage. Forget yourselves long enough to lend a helping hand.
Philippians 2:3-4 (MSG)

We are God's handiwork, created in Christ Jesus to do good works, which God prepared in advance for us to do.
Ephesians 2:10 (NIV)

Many are the plans in a person's heart, but it is the Lord's purpose that prevails.
Proverbs 19:21 (NIV)

Step 12
Lack to Life: Experiencing Fulfillment

● ● ● ● ● ● ● ● ● ● ● ● ● ● ●

Lack means being without.

Life is the ability to grow or change.

Today's society is laser-focused on more, better, and bigger: more clothes, a better job, a bigger house, and an even bigger bank account!

While I had everything society said I should have: a loving family, supportive friends, a spiritual community, and a steady career, feelings of unfulfillment seemed to be lurking around every corner. The state of being without had nothing to do with material possessions or relationships and everything to do with my life lacking purpose. There was a void that I learned could never be filled without allowing myself to be my authentic self and experience life to its fullest.

God has so many blessings in life for us; however, fear and lack of trust in Him often hold us back. A balance of mental, emotional, physical, and spiritual growth is critical in experiencing fulfillment in our lives.

Give yourself permission to live free. Free from fear of other people's opinions. Free from the need for validation and approval.

Free to feel your emotions, and free to be yourself. Create healthy boundaries, be kind to yourself, spend time alone, and spend time with God.

In the words of a dear friend, *"You gotta stay in life!"*

"Christ has set us free to live a free life. So, take your stand! Never again let anyone put a harness of slavery on you."
Galatians 5:1 (MSG)

Reflection Questions for the Journey

1) How does fear hold you back from experiencing life to its fullest?

_____
_____
_____
_____
_____
_____
_____
_____
_____
_____
_____
_____
_____
_____
_____
_____
_____
_____
_____
_____
_____
_____
_____
_____
_____
_____
_____
_____
_____
_____
_____
_____
_____

2) In what ways can a focus on your spiritual growth remove lack from your life?

_____
_____
_____
_____
_____
_____
_____
_____
_____
_____
_____
_____
_____
_____
_____
_____
_____
_____
_____
_____
_____
_____
_____
_____
_____
_____
_____
_____

Step 12

Scriptures to Guide Your Self-Love Journey

Delight yourself in the Lord, and he will give you the desires of your heart.
Psalm 37:4 (ESV)

But seek first his kingdom and his righteousness, and all these things will be given to you as well.
Matthew 6:33 (NIV)

You make known to me the path of life; in your presence there is fullness of joy; at your right hand are pleasures forevermore.
Psalm 16:11 (ESV)

Christ has set us free to live a free life. So, take your stand! Never again let anyone put a harness of slavery on you.
Galatians 5:1 (MSG)

Hope deferred makes the heart sick, but a longing fulfilled is a tree of life.
Proverbs 13:12 (NIV)

Conclusion

What a journey it has been! From there to here. From here to there. From lack to life. Making connections. Bridging gaps. Learning and growing.

 The journey to self-love begins and ends with celebrating YOU! The Old Testament book, Zephaniah 3:17 (GW), tells us: *"The Lord your God is with you. He is a hero who saves you. He happily rejoices over you, renews you with his love, and celebrates over you with shouts of joy."*

So, go ahead and celebrate YOU – God does!

I pray that as you begin (or continue) your journey, you have been blessed by mine.

As you take the next steps on your own, remember that you have worth and value because of Him.

Share Your Thoughts

● ● ● ● ● ● ● ● ● ● ● ● ● ●

If this book blessed you, please consider taking 2 minutes to leave a review so others can be encouraged too. Your review will:

- help the woman struggling to put herself first and know that self care isn't selfish
- encourage the believer who hasn't quite mastered saying no
- let others know this is the book they need to put their faith into action for more intentional self-care

To get started, open the camera app on your smartphone, and place it over the image to leave a review on Amazon. Or simply visit amazon.com and locate the book on the site.

Acknowledgments

• • • • • • • • • • • • • •

I am deeply grateful to so many for the support, love, and guidance along my journey to self-love and authoring my first book.

I am *forever indebted* to my dear friend and brother-in-Christ, Reverend Victor Ray Wade, who with care and consistency, listened to me, prayed with me, prayed for me, counseled me, and even admonished me, as needed.

I am *forever grateful* for my precious and loyal *"sister circle"* (*you know who you are*) for always believing in me, encouraging me, supporting me, and reminding me…YOU CAN DO THIS!

I am *forever beholden* to my brother and sister-in-love, Herbert and June Latney, for being on my side with an undying love that can never be expressed solely in words.

I am *forever in love* with my sons, Reginald II and Ryan, who always said, "Go for it, Mommy!"

Finally, I am *forever duty-bound* to give all thanks and praise to God, for He is certainly worthy of being praised!

About the Author

• • • • • • • • • • • • • •

As a Certified Life Coach, Board Certified Mental Health Coach, Pastoral Counselor, and Temperament Counselor, Cheryl L. Bridges offers support through temperament coaching and other strategies designed to uncover any unmet needs that often cause stress and conflict in life and relationships. Cheryl comes alongside clients to help increase their self-esteem and clarify their vision and direction to unlock their potential.

Cheryl is also the founder and CEO of Bridges 2 Life, a faith-based coaching organization created to offer support to individuals, families and communities while working together to build bridges to a better life through spiritual coaching, temperament counseling and training, group coaching sessions, self-esteem workshops, and much more. Cheryl's primary goal is to help her coaching clients grow in their spiritual walk by embracing self-love and provide feedback to assist their walk through life's transitions.

About Bridges 2 Life

● ● ● ● ● ● ● ● ● ● ● ● ● ●

Connecting who you are to who you want to be

Bridges 2 Life, LLC is a faith-based coaching organization created to offer support to individuals, families, and communities. We work diligently to build bridges to a better life through Christian/spiritual coaching, temperament counseling and training, group coaching sessions, self-esteem workshops, and more.

Our primary goal is to help you experience growth in your spiritual walk while embracing God's love for you. Bridges 2 Life will assist you in connecting who you are to who you want to be by identifying your God-given, inborn temperament, understanding the strengths, weaknesses, and needs of your character, and modifying your behaviors with the Holy Spirit as your guide. God wants you to THRIVE, not just survive – even amid struggles and challenges that can stand in your way. Despite it all, you are enough, and our God is MORE than enough!

Our Services:

• Wellness/Life Coaching

• Temperament Counseling and Workshops

• Pre-Marital & Couple Services

For more information, visit www.Bridges2Life.com. To connect with Cheryl and find out more ways to practice self care, follow her on Instagram, Facebook, and YouTube @Bridges2Life.

To get started, open the camera app on your smartphone, and place it over the image.

Notes for Your Self-Love Journey

Notes for Your Self-Love Journey

Notes for Your Self-Love Journey

Notes for Your Self-Love Journey

Notes for Your Self-Love Journey

Notes for Your Self-Love Journey

Printed in Great Britain
by Amazon

40936233R00046